Snap
books

DRAWING
Your Pets

BY **ABBY COLICH**   ILLUSTRATED BY **STEFANO AZZALIN**

raintree
a Capstone company — publishers for children

Raintree is an imprint of Capstone Global Library Limited, a company incorporated in England and Wales having its registered office at 7 Pilgrim Street, London, EC4V 6LB – Registered company number: 6695582

www.raintree.co.uk
myorders@raintree.co.uk

Edited by Abby Colich

Designed by Juliette Peters and Charmaine Whitman

Cover designed by Aruna Rangarajan

Illustrated by Juan Calle

Production by Laura Manthe

ISBN 978 1 4062 9435 4
18 17 16 15 14
10 9 8 7 6 5 4 3 2 1

British Library Cataloguing in Publication Data

A full catalogue record for this book is available from the British Library.

Printed and bound in China.

Contents

Getting started

From brightly coloured betta fish to playful puppies, the world is full of amazing pets. Pets are fun to learn about and fun to draw, too. Whether you're skilled at sketching or new to the world of drawing, you can have fun filling pages with a wide variety of pets.

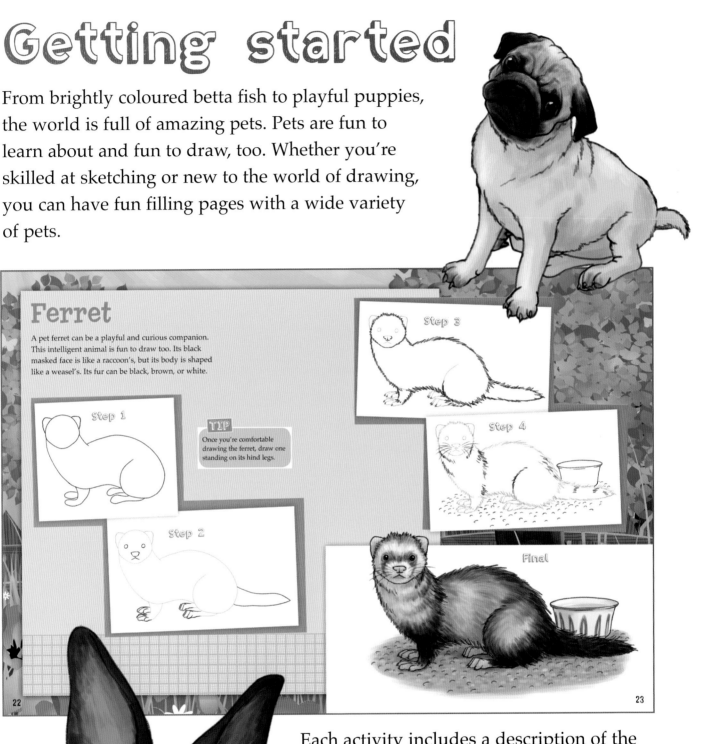

Ferret

A pet ferret can be a playful and curious companion. This intelligent animal is fun to draw too. Its black masked face is like a raccoon's, but its body is shaped like a weasel's. Its fur can be black, brown, or white.

Step 1

Step 2

Step 3

Step 4

Final

TIP
Once you're comfortable drawing the ferret, draw one standing on its hind legs.

22

23

Each activity includes a description of the animal, steps to show you exactly how to draw each pet, and a tip for when you want to get creative and try something new. If your hamster looks horrible or your ferret is flawed, don't worry. Drawing takes practice. If you make a mistake, it's OK to start again. Just remember to be creative and have fun while you work.

Tools of the trade

Drawing is a fun and inexpensive way to express yourself and your creativity. Before you get started, make sure you have the proper tools.

Paper

Any white paper will work, but a sketchbook specifically for drawing is best.

Pencils

Any pencil will do, but many artists prefer graphite pencils made especially for drawing.

Colour

A good set of coloured pencils will give you many options for colour. You can also try using felt-tip pens or paint. Many artists enjoy outlining and filling in their work with artist pens.

Sharpener

Your pencils will be getting a lot of use, so make sure you have a sturdy sharpener. A good sharpener will give your pencil a nice, sharp point.

Rubber

Be sure to get a good rubber. Choose a rubber that won't leave smudges on your clean, white paper.

Drawing on screen

Many great apps and computer programs allow you to draw on screen rather than on paper. If you want to give this medium a try, ask an adult to help you get started. Learn all the features and functions before you begin.

Betta fish

Betta fish, also known as Siamese fighting fish, might be aggressive to other fish, but they are lovely to watch. These fish come in many gorgeous colours, including shades of orange, red, blue and green. You can capture their vibrant colours best when you draw their large, flowing fins extended outwards.

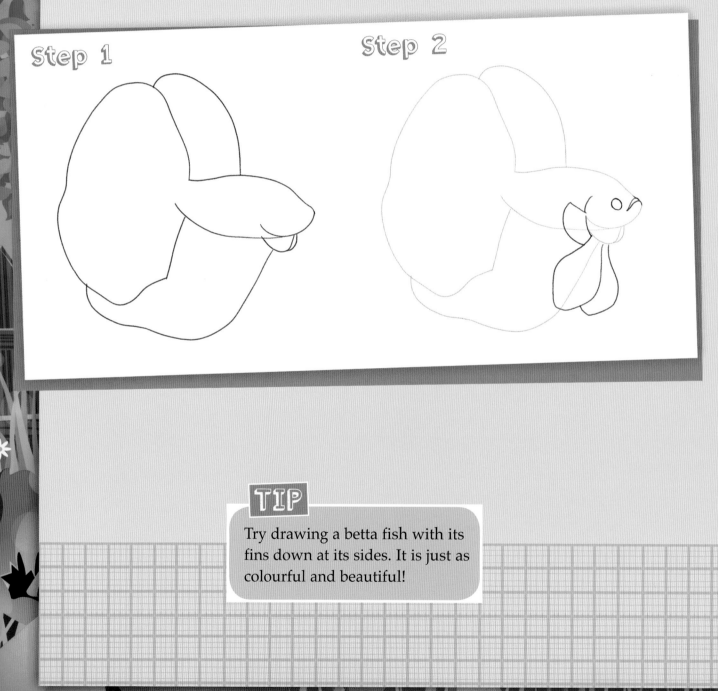

Step 1

Step 2

TIP

Try drawing a betta fish with its fins down at its sides. It is just as colourful and beautiful!

Step 3

Step 4

Final

Hamster

The cute and fluffy hamster is so small it can fit in the palm of your hand. These rodents can be a variety of sizes and colours. Its paws look like tiny hands. Don't forget that detail when drawing this fun pet.

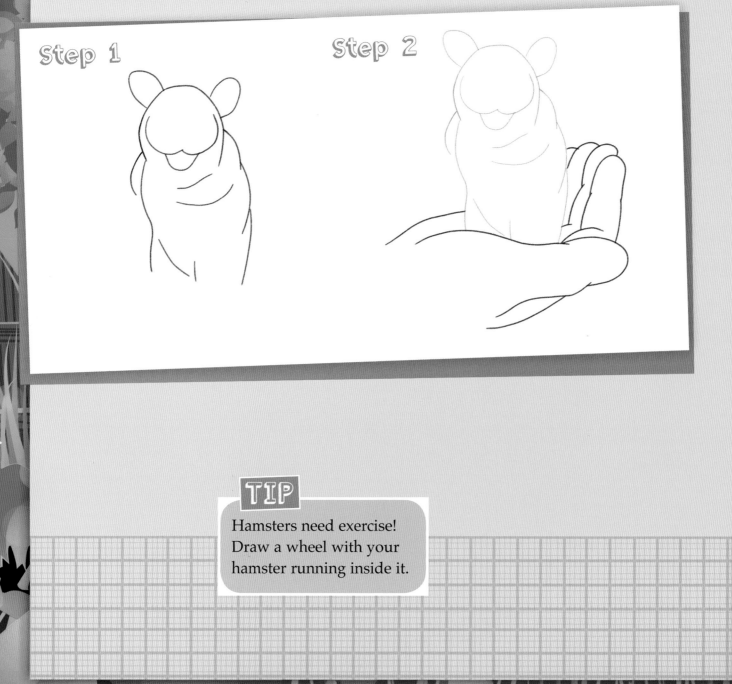

Step 1

Step 2

TIP

Hamsters need exercise! Draw a wheel with your hamster running inside it.

Step 3

Step 4

Final

Tree frog

Tree frogs have to be kept wet, but you can stay dry
while drawing this amazing amphibian. Have fun as
you fill in the neon green body, blue markings, red
eyes and orange feet.

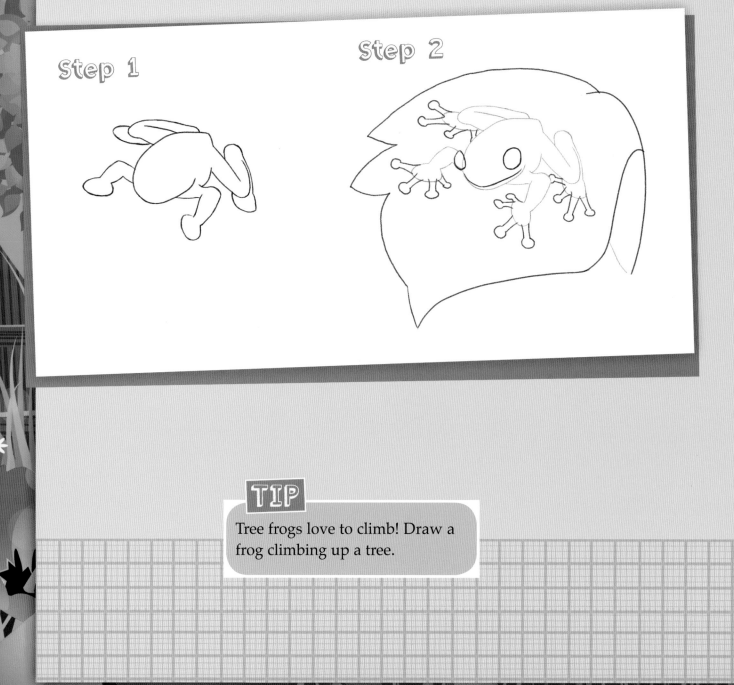

Step 1

Step 2

TIP

Tree frogs love to climb! Draw a
frog climbing up a tree.

Step 3

Step 4

Final

Parrot

The parrot is the only pet you can teach your language! Whether perched in its cage or on your shoulder, a parrot may want to chat as you sketch. Be sure to draw the beak curved and pointed. This feature helps the parrot to crack open hard nuts.

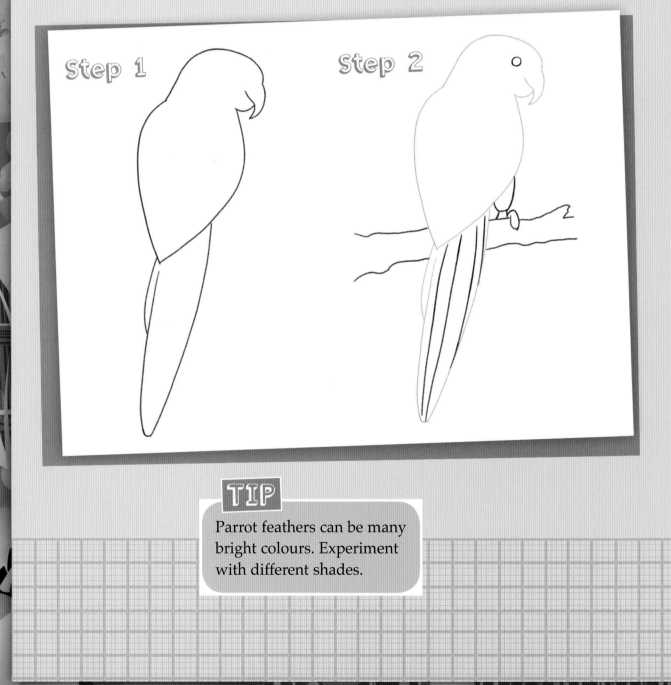

Step 1

Step 2

TIP

Parrot feathers can be many bright colours. Experiment with different shades.

Step 3

Step 4

Final

Rabbit

A pet rabbit is cute and cuddly. Even though your paper and pencil aren't soft and furry, you can still have fun drawing this pet! Its floppy ears and cotton-like tail may be your favourite features, but don't forget the whiskers!

TIP

Pet rabbits like to run around on the grass. Draw your rabbit playing in the garden.

Step 3

Step 4

Final

Cat

Cats are playful and mischievous creatures. They'll scurry across the floor chasing their toys, hide in a corner and jump from high spaces. Then they'll curl up next to you for a nap. Capture the amazing life of a pet cat with this sketch.

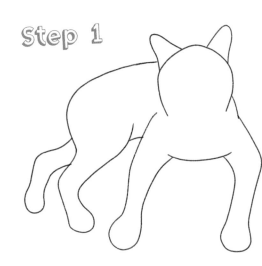

Step 1

Step 2

TIP

Cats always land on their feet when jumping from high spaces. Try capturing your cat making a smooth landing.

Step 3

Step 4

Final

Pug with puppies

Sketch these dogs with their wrinkly faces, boxy bodies and curly tails. Most pugs have light brown (fawn) fur, but they can also be black, grey or white. The puppies are like miniature versions of the adults!

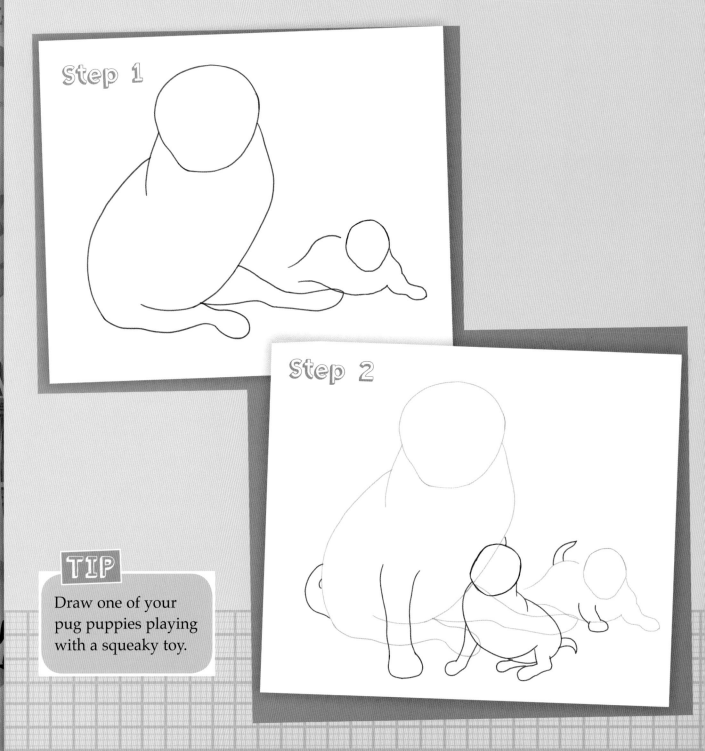

Step 1

Step 2

TIP
Draw one of your pug puppies playing with a squeaky toy.

Step 3

Step 4

continued on next page

Step 5

Step 6

Final

Ferret

A pet ferret can be a playful and curious companion. This intelligent animal is fun to draw, too. Its black masked face is like a raccoon's, but its body is shaped like a weasel's. Its fur can be black, brown or white.

Step 1

Step 2

TIP

Once you're comfortable drawing the ferret, draw one standing on its hind legs.

Step 3

Step 4

Final

Horse

Shiny, beautiful hair growing from a long, flowing mane is just one majestic quality of the horse. A horse's personality shows through in its facial expressions. When you recreate this beautiful animal on paper, try to catch it in its graceful gallop.

Step 1

Step 2

TIP

Once you master the horse, add a saddle and reins.

Step 3

Step 4

continued on next page

25

Step 5

Step 6

Final

Tropical fish tank

Colourful fish swimming to and fro. Plants swaying back and forth. A starfish resting on the rocks. Put this beautiful scene together by drawing a tropical fish tank. Take your time sketching the details, and have fun filling in the colours.

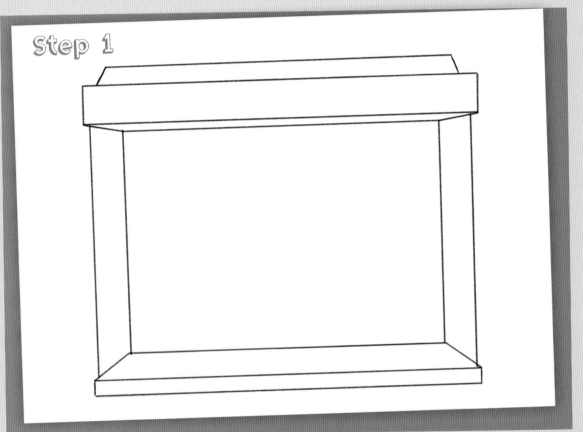

Step 1

TIP

Do you know how to draw any other fish tank creatures? Perhaps a shrimp or a little eel? Try adding these to your tank.

Step 2

Step 3

continued on next page

Final

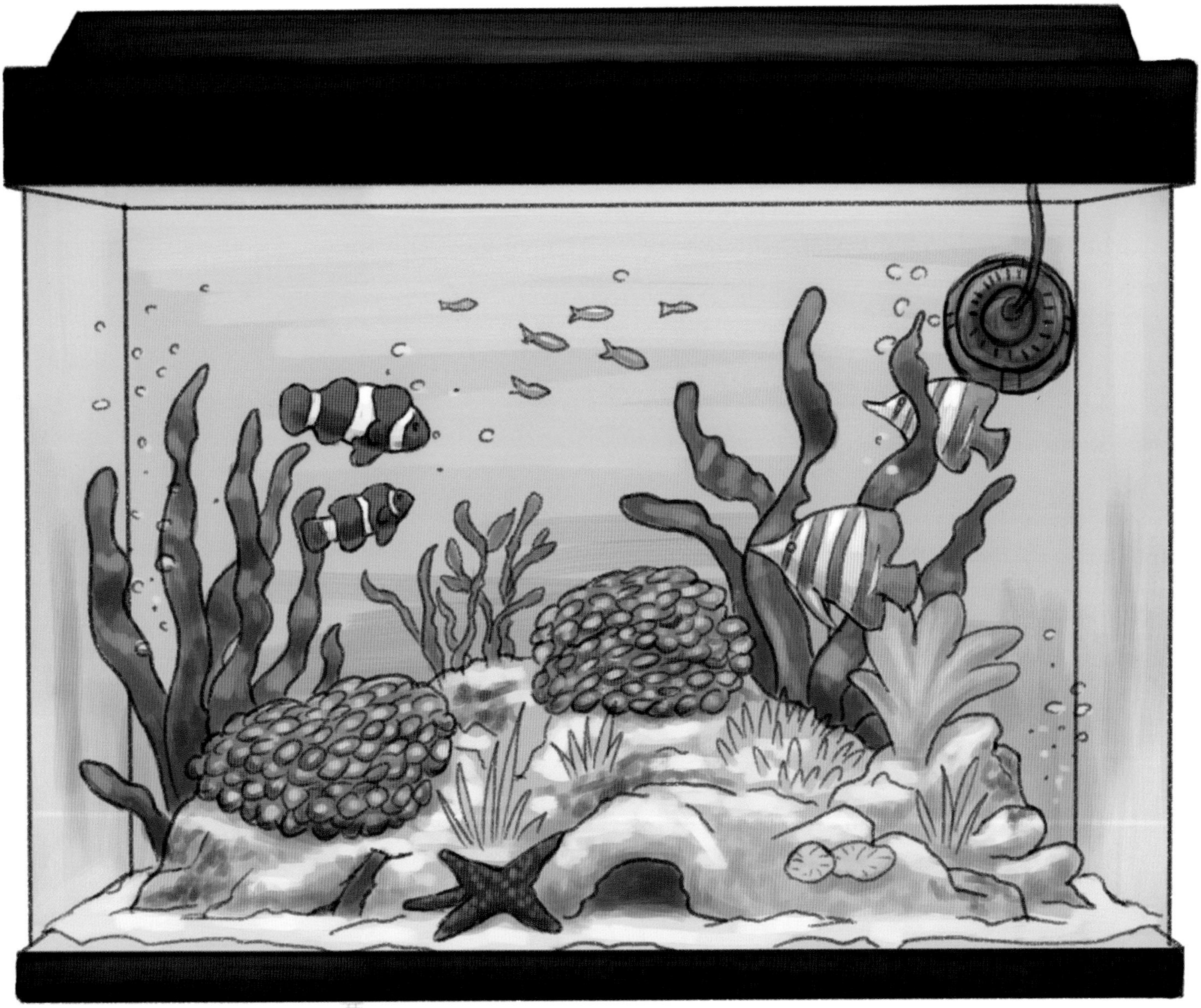

Websites

www.bbc.co.uk/education/topics/zwc4jxs

Get creative! From pencils and inks to digital design tools, find hints and tips, including video demonstrations, for using all types of media and materials for your artwork.

www.bbc.co.uk/nature/animals/

Get inspired! Find hundreds of beautiful photographs and videos of the world's most amazing wild animals and try your hand at drawing them!

www.theguardian.com/childrens-books-site/series/how-to-draw

Learn from the experts! Follow these step-by-step guides and learn how to draw some of your favourite characters.

Look for all the books in this series!

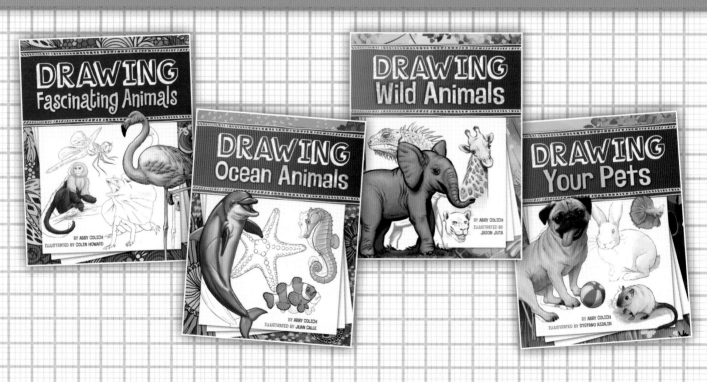